MAPS OF A WORLD

Poems, Prose, and Stories

JENNIFER MALONEY

Raw Earth Ink

2025

*For the once-upon-a-time
children of Galena Street,
with all my love*

This book is a work of poetry.

Copyright 2025 by Jennifer Maloney

All rights reserved. No part of this book may be reproduced or used in any manner without express written permission from the author except in the case of quotations used in a book review in which a clear link to the source of the quote and its author is required.

First paperback edition November 2025

ISBN 978-1-960991-56-0 (paperback)

Published by Raw Earth Ink
PO Box 2
Humboldt, IA 50548
www.raw-earth-ink.com

Table of Contents

1968 2
Maps of a World 4
Galena Street II 6
God of My Father 9
Galena Street 12
Dirty Summer 14
Christmas Visit 17
Dream Christine 19
The Day and I 21
How We Go 22
Elegy for a Fairy Tale 24
To Grandmother's House 26
Unchanged 28
What Already Could Be Written No More* 30
Cousinweed 33
Celebration 35
Secret Lives of Small Things 37
Galena Street III 39
Acknowledgements 41
About the Author 42

1968

Here it is: the polka-dot umbrella, the clear-plastic sixties—boots and raincoat and purse—yes, look inside, here are the squeezable lips of a change purse, here is its keychain with its little silver beads. Look inside, we are transparent, here are our beautiful, unimpugnable thoughts, perfect and pure. Look at us, my mother and I, as we walk down Leroy Street on our way to the bus stop, perfect and pure, mother and child. The neighbors see our purity through our clear plastic. Under our layers of transparency, sheathed in raindrops, above reflective puddles, of course they can see us. The neighbors see everything, like x-ray machines, right down to every break and fracture because we are clear as rain. Surely, they see my brother's arm, caught in the wringer in the cellar. See the words we've written on our skin in ash, in smoke, rising, disappearing. Everything is clear. Look, she holds our hands, look, she grips our arms, look, we never run screaming into the street. Clearly, we are in no danger. Danger is written large, in red, it flashes, but everything here is clear and calm. The puddles, smooth as mirrors, have nothing to reflect because the neighbors can see through it all and have raised the all-clear.

***

The moon is a hanged man in the sky, slowly disappearing, rotting away, until all that is left is a sliver of bone. Count the days on your fingers, your fingers of bone—as though you, too, have rotted away. When will you disappear?

***

Soft, feet as quiet as moonlight patter up and down a stair. We don't know who travels there, or if they, also, are slowly disappearing into transparency. Clarity. The all-clear of our neighbors' 20/20 eyesight, perfect, pure, their vision unobscured, as see-through as 1968.

Maps of a World

Any map of the neighborhood has to include the hiding spots. The green room that sways under the weeping willow with walls like hula dancers in their rustling grass skirts. The fence between yards with a hidden gate, a secret to creep through. The silence that fills my bladder, the pressure, burn and squeeze a strangely pleasurable secret beneath pink cotton shorts, other secrets beneath t-shirt and socks, the invisible map of my body. My father blows in my ear and a wave of goosepimples rides from the bottoms of my feet to the back of my neck. My legs, adding inches in the night, stretching and aching. Mosquitos suck at my scalp—I scratch those secrets until they ooze, harden like sap, yellow as globs of honey stuck to the red-lacquer bark of the cherry tree, peeling, translucent, the box I buried beneath its roots rattling with baby teeth and old keys and holiest of holies, a stolen matchbook. A martini glass with stuffed olive eyes stumbles on its cover in tippy heels, splashing, sloshing, brandishing a tiny red sword, flushed and giggling, a secret on its breath, a gleaming secret in its eyes. What did it mean?

Any map of the neighborhood must include the danger spots. Past the jingling chain link at the back of Grandma's yard, the little grove of pines whose soft floor is dotted with old beer bottles filled with urine. The boy who lives there pisses in them, throws them into the miniature wood. Cushioned atop fragrant red needles, they land unbroken but leaking filth into his unclaimed Eden. He's big, a teenager, he scares us— once, while we waited for the school bus, he shoved a lit cigarette between my lips. Its cherry-red end blossomed like a signal-flare, laying us bare, uncovering all the hot and precious things we kept crushed beneath our eyelids, and I stood there, stuck as sap, as if I had no hands, as if the keys I'd hidden had locked my lungs and elbows, only my eyes moved, jumping from face to face, all of us stopped, waiting for me to scream, or spit, or — suck? What happened next? Any map of the neighborhood must include the spaces I left blank inside my head.

Galena Street II

I am down Galena Street—it's summer,
Bev's beautiful mother sings opera
that flutters out windows like feathers—
like a molt
from her dust mop—

Bev and I are July-brown—
brown skin,
brown eyes, brown hair—
white teeth—
one missing—

arias wing over empty sills,
billow past dramatic curtains,
uncurl down Galena Street
like slender tongues—her long throat lifts,
a beat trills there—
such an unexpected bird,
so far from home—

                        other mothers lifting brows,
                        lifting coffee in our kitchen—

Bev's big brother blocks the door,
knuckle-punches, ponytail pulls,
squeezes hard against me
squeezing past—

her mother crescendos—

and every morning like the moon,
Bev's father fades like all the fathers,
furloughed to Saturdays,
available for R&R,
otherwise AWOL —
a mutineer —

        and mothers in our kitchen mutter
        nervous break down
        put away
        chins and eyebrows jerk at me
        are you sure you ought to...?

When Bev's sister lipsticks our teeth,
shadows our eyes as blue as veins,
my mother says a word
that I don't know, scrubs my face,
dials the phone —
instead of walking down the street,
she dials the phone —
the numbers grind
around its face — *click-tick-tick*
like sand — she dials the phone,
calls someone not Bev's mother —

        her hair-bowed, pedal-
      pushed mother,
           her ballet-flats-or-
      barefoot mother,
           her sings-along-with-
      records mother —
           Carmen,
           La Bohème,
           The Magic Flute —

***

at the dead-end of Galena Street,
the gulley looms behind the rail,
and Bev and her beautiful mother,
her pretty sister, her mean brother,
live nearer,
much nearer
that hole
than I —

                              and her father
                              has deserted his post —

God of My Father

God of my father,
pen-and-ink god,
cross-hatched and black, rockpile god,
a cloud hangs above like a convict,
the sun looms and streams
nineteenth-century glory,
stylized rays, a warden eye.
God of my father
speaks in red proclamations
that leech to the edge of onionskin pages,
blood-stained as a crime-scene, murderer god
zipped into a mouthful of gold metal teeth.
No one comes to my childhood a tourist.

High walls of dank apple trees
rot and ferment,
hard yellow ice in a cow creek moat.
On visiting days,
my aunts drag their husbands
who slouch and eyeroll,
check watches, drum fingers.
My mother slaps food on the table,
a dare. Slumps into a chair,
loud whoosh from her lungs and her seat,
her big bottom lapping its edges.

Aunts' pressurized chatter,
fingers flutter, palms nervous,
smooth tablecloths, hair, conversations.
Mother's corpse-crossed arms,
her lemonsuck mouth,

anger banked like a fire,
saved like old coins,
safe-deposit-box anger,
unmarked bearer bonds,
and the god of my father a criminal, thief,
a safecracker, arsonist god —
sequestered in solitary confinement —
quarantined in the black leather bible —
hidden in the drawer
at the top of the hutch
beneath shivering brass
and quavering glass,
talks to itself like a madman,
chitters and buzzes and squawks.
No one comes to my childhood on vacation.
No one visits without obligation.

No getaway drivers, so no jailbreaks,
there is no good behavior, no sentences shortened,
all of us lifers, each one condemned,
and the god of my father ticks like a clock
and my mother is wired like plastic explosives
and the countdown is lurching
and rolling and winding,
speeding and stopping
and clicking and flashing,
as my aunts try to talk the bomb
out of exploding,
push the pin
back in
the grenade.
If you come to my childhood a tourist,
you will leave it a refugee.

If you come as a hostage negotiator,
you will leave with blood on your hands.

Come to disarm the bomb,
or don't come at all,
the god of my father is striking the match,
my mother bends to the fuse.

Galena Street

Streetlight on snow, nothing is colder. Industrial yellow light, smell of burning wire, railroad tracks, transformers, my father holds my brother's face against a table, green as felt, green as spruce trees, wet with tears.

I know what it is to be a prisoner, don't say I don't. I know how to long. How to count. How to wait with my mouth squeezed tight, tight. A white line wriggles across my face like a grub. Caught by the crow. A delicacy.

Our doctor's office. Pebbled stone castle under shaggy spruce trees, friendly as old dogs. Carved wooden toys with carved wooden wheels. Walks into the exam room. Stops. *Why did you take your underwear off?*

I thought you would want me this way.

At home the hutch rattles, chatters like it's cold, small brass handles tap brass plates. Inside drawers, smell of cedar, pipe tobacco. A book, cloth binding the color of old blood wrapped around monsters that swallow children whole. *Wigwam Tales*. Trace the words that hold the worlds.

The bath gleams, fluorescent. Everything stinks of Lysol, bleach, hard enough to crack a head, break a finger, operating-room-white. Chrome fixtures flash like surgical instruments.

Grandma lives across the street in a cottage that puffs purple smoke from the chimney. A steam engine. Friendly.

Daddy's trains are electric. Click and oil around the tracks, cinch tight the green-floored town, its roads, streetlamps, stink of burn and melt.

What is the truth? Broken fingers, friendly smoke? Cracked heads and naked children, unburnt tobacco, nervous brass handles?

It's cold in hell, having frozen over. Under jaundiced light, the whirr and clatter of tracks, cold. You can smell the burning, but you can't get warm.

Out front the hedges grow fat, red berries, food for birds that gather on evergreen branches, green as spruce trees, green as felt. They eat their fill, then fly to our roof, pass over the car and shit on it, a beautiful purple stream.

My father fills his pipe, philosophical. *We feed and clothe the things that turn on us, don't we?* muses my father.

Dirty Summer

She comes every June to set us free. Zooms into our neat little neighborhood, somehow boiling a cloud of dust from Grandma's swept asphalt, brakes squealing like a stunt driver. Grandma's jaw works but she forces the corners of her mouth up, tries to smile a welcome. The car fishtails in, parks crooked as a middle finger. A naked brown foot, toenails the color of a freshly skinned knee, heels open the driver's door and a cardboard cup in a long-fingered hand appears. Immediately upends. A brown waterfall of liquid and half-melted ice splatters the driveway, and as it rivers down to the street I hear it: that wonderful voice. *Yuck, flat,* Aunt Glory announces, and summer begins.

Her voice! Her voice *is* summer: LonG Island laid-back. The crackle of Coca-Cola in a rock glass tilting gently south accompanies it like music. Leaned back in a webbed lawn chair, long, freckled arms drag a cigarette dangerously close to the brown brush-cut of Grandma's lawn, threaten to set it alight, one bare foot swinging lazy as a loose shutter in an ocean breeze. She says *Why worry? I nevah do,* and you know that's the absolute truth. After so many buttoned-up months, it's time to loosen our collars. After so much clean, it's time to get dirty again.

She decides to drive us to the beach, her natural habitat. She invites Grandma, who shakes her head, looking at her with that squeezed look she gets around the eyes when Aunt Glory blows in, like she's trying to read something without her glasses. *Suit yaself,* shrugs Aunt Glory, opening the door to the big backseat and bowing to us like she's the head waiter at a fancy restaurant.

We yell and pile into the car, toting a beach bag full of bath towels and dry clothes and a Styrofoam cooler stuffed with tuna fish sandwiches and cans of Orange Crush that Grandma packed. Next to Aunt Glory's hip, her purse overflows with a bottle of tanning oil, a hairbrush, and at least three open packs of cigarettes. Grandma leans in the front window as Aunt Glory starts the car, pins her with a serious look. *You be careful*, she says, jerking her head towards us, and even though I can't see it I know Aunt Glory is rolling her eyes as she lights her first Salem of the trip. *Mom*, she mutters around it, exasperated, *stop worrying!* and we reverse down the driveway, lurching hard into drive at the bottom, the three of us in the backseat sliding around on the white leather like pinballs, knocking into each other, gasping and laughing and hollering out the open windows, on our way. Aunt Glory rummages around in her purse and I hear the crack and hiss of a can opening. She raises it to her lips. I look back at Grandma standing at the top of the driveway, arms folded, watching us leave, and a cigarette is hanging from her lips, too, so out of place I almost gasp. It stutters up and down like it's trembling, and my stomach grabs the way it does when I try to tell her a lie, and none of it makes sense so I forget it.

What's the good station? Aunt Glory yells over the rush of wind. *BBF, BBF!* We holler back, and almost immediately the Beach Boys spill out of the radio's speakers, flood the car, pour out its windows. Susie and Nance and I start singing *Wouldn't it be Nice* at the top of our lungs and the back of Aunt Glory's blonde head bobs along in time. *Wouldn't it be nice if we were older? Then we wouldn't have to wait so long...*

We scatter the gulls from the beach parking lot as we roar in. Doors bang open, slam shut, my sisters run toward the sand. Aunt Glory totters along behind us, purse and beach bag slung over shoulders, struggling with the cooler, a lot heavier since she opened the trunk and stuck something else in it. I head back to take it from her, and she hesitates briefly, then ruffles my hair. *Yer tha best, honey,* she tells me in her summer voice, full of sunshine and smoke, already a little blurred at the edges and starting to fade...

...but maybe that's just my untrustworthy memory. I can't remember my sisters' voices except in dreams, singing about wishing they didn't have to wait so long to be older, not knowing they wouldn't have to wait any longer at all, so why should I remember Aunt Glory's so perfectly? Why do I know the exact moment she got dirty again, after all those months of being clean?

Christmas Visit

Grandpa Gene is feeding me cream soda in the apartment on Cayuga Street, the downstairs apartment, the one with French doors that lead into their bedroom. It's a treat so I will nap. *Cream soda is root beer only better,* I think out the window. *Mr. Pibb is Dr. Pepper and Squirt is Fresca. Orange Crush doesn't taste like anything else, but it stings. Hurts.* I squinch up my eyes like Orange Crush.

There's a white chenille bedspread, nubbly and fringed, scented with mothballs and Aqua Velva. Outside, lamplight brightens winter trees whose gray arms sway and shake their fists, throw fat, wet snowballs into the street. Their roots are gnarled as Grandpa's feet, claw into iced-over snow, black with the soot of passing cars that roll in a slow parade on their way to midnight mass. White-leather topped, gold-and-chrome sided, they look like Father Michael processing to the altar, ignoring everyone around him, holy and focused. I try to stay holy and focused but I keep looking at the clock, its green glowing numbers, wondering how long it will be before we go to church, too, climb into Grandpa's car, its inside hot and red as his mouth, smelling of hard-bit cee-gars.

I hear my mother arrive. I get up and run back through the French doors. Perched on the wingback, black coffee in hand, her penciled brows wing up, swoop down as I come in, a red paisley kerchief bowing her hair. At home, she is pin curls and a housecoat, but here she is always drawn up and tied tight, although there is a little pink stain on the rim of her cup.

A small plastic tree, green as a toad, squats in the living room window. I stretch a shred of silver foil over one of its hot, blue bulbs. Watch it melt. Grandpa swats my bottom with a rolled-up National Geographic. Winks. *What were you doing in there?* asks my mother.

Grandma Nancy bakes thumbprint cookies while a cigarette droops from the side of her mouth, squinting one eye. Yellow butter mints in a cut glass bowl melt creamy-cold in my mouth, peppery with ash. Doilies spot tables, chair-backs; Grandpa's hair pomade stains just like lipstick. *Why were they in there?* Grandma shrugs, the cigarette bouncing as she bends to the oven.

I said no naps with him, my mother hisses. Grandma picks me up and sets me in a kitchen chair, hands me a still-warm cookie. Pops open another bottle of soda. It exhales like a satisfied man. *You can have anything you want, Honey,* says Grandma, *don't mind your mother*

who picks up her coffee and drinks it like she's stopping a scream, the rim of her cup stained, the bottom of my shirt stained, all of us a mess and still having to go to mass.

Dream Christine

Dream Christine is a marionette. She bobbles and clacks. Wobbles. Floats.

Dream Christine calls me. Voice on the phone crinkles like aluminum foil. *I'm not dead,* says Dream Christine. *I need my car.*

and now I am in her car, her big Oldsmobile, driving it to her, to where she is hiding. When I arrive, she drifts out, hanging from her strings. Her elbows hinge, unhinge, her toes scrape the earth, scritch-scritch. *Thank you,* she says, jaw flapping, *but this isn't really me.*

What's going on? I ask, and her painted smile tips sideways, wooden finger raises. *Ssshh,* says Dream Christine, *no telling,* and then she is gone, because dreams end mid-sentence just like life.

Heroin, methadone, a bucket of brains. A nursery rhyme of ways to die, join hands children, dance.

On Galena Street, it was always summer, and even if it wasn't, it was better outside. The maple tree, Bev and Erin, ring around the rosy. Daddy's home. Home safe. Everyone understood.

Like everyone else, I don't understand love, but I know what it smells like: the lemon-dab of Jean Naté The storage room at church where we tried on other people's clothes, musty, mildew. Dust in the filtered sunlight of the afternoon living room, the slow tick of punishment, the smell of my own snot and tears stopped up in my throat. Melting plastic. Love smells like grief. No one understands but everyone knows.

Once I had a little puppet, white-blond hair, a polka-dot pinafore. I hid her in the playhouse to keep her safe, but we were found out. Grief melts like plastic. Scissors into ribbons, a heap on the floor. *Clean it up.* Nobody knew.

Dream Christine's hair is red, but she has a puppet's face, black eyes and painted smile. *Don't tell,* whispers Dream Christine, pirouetting on her strings, pinafore twirling. *I won't,* I promise.

The Day and I

Words slide up my leg like a silk slip. Like the hand beneath the slip that drifts to my collarbone, plays love notes on my neck like a piano, percussive. I shiver. Wake up falling. Try to stand but darkness slams me against the wall. My eyes tick, tick, tick like a second hand. The word is nystagmus. The word is concussion. The word is vertigo. There are white spaces between words, places to rest, as though I could rest. Pull them apart, they unravel like an old sweater, the daylight between them illuminates nothing. The day stands in the doorway, uncertain, eyes stumbling from face to face. Someone sighs. No one speaks. My eyes swing like a pendulum as the day wrings its hands—I am dizzy, falling backwards between the car's front seats, you and the day holding me, kissing me, fingers purpling words into my throat, I am floating, wondering if I like them, knowing that I do, these words like *bruise*, like *busted*, like *broken*, like I'm six again on Galena Street where the door is a window and it must be the sun that blinds me, trips me, shoves me right through, I feel its hot, hard hand against my back. I fall into the day, into its arms, spilling a message on the front step. The doctor says *stitches*. My mother says *clumsy*. The day and I don't say a word.

How We Go

Under the sun, all details erase. My fingers twine, the light between them, diffuse, glowing through the thin skin that divides them, through my eyelids, pulse and pressure. In my grandmother's car, red leather, black dash, my hands between me and the sun. At the top of her windshield the glass turns green. Deepens. An egg-shaped compass floats and wobbles on the dashboard.

My grandmother, driving us to Star Market, Mother simmering in the seat next to her. Grandma's cigarette wedged at the ashtray's edge, pink lip-print trembling like it might cry. My mother's cigarette ribboning smoke out her window, her white plastic cat's eye sunglasses winging up in perpetual dismay, their lenses green as the top of the windshield, a red paisley kerchief knotted beneath her chin rippling in the breeze and nobody's talking. Two sets of bow-shaped lips, one pink, one red, one pointed staunchly toward the road, one twisted towards the window, sipping smoke, fuming.

At the grocery store Grandma will pull up in the fire lane. My mother will slam out, fling open my door, yank me from the red leather into which I've been trying to shrink, to burrow, grab my upper arm and pull me out onto the pavement, hip-shut the car door and drag me away, tossing *we'll walk home* over her shoulder at Grandma, who won't hear, already pulling out in a screech of burnt rubber and hurt feelings. I'll stumble along in my mother's grip, past glass globes filled with pastel jawbreakers, SweetTarts and mouse turds, my arm bruising beneath her fingers, the sun unable to erase those shadows.

The cart bites my thighs, pinch and scratch. I want to stand on the back and ride like the big kids, but she won't let me. Squirm, wiggle, try not to cry, bite the inside of my lip to stop it, but my face is still something she can police and she slaps it. *Quit it!* A hiss under her breath. *Don't you dare embarrass me,* but now I can't stop, I can't, the sun is in my eyes again, glowing, stinging, erasing every barrier.

Finally, she lifts me out. *Fine, get down,* she sneers, *but it's sure gonna be a long walk home, Sunshine.* I don't care because the grocery store is cool, green as celery, yellow as bananas, there are big, pillowy letters hanging on the walls that I can't read but red and blue balloons mean Wonder Bread, my nails scratch paths in the milk carton's wax, and the eggs in their baby blue Styrofoam beds remind me of the compass in Grandma's car. I like the compass, but it tattles. It tells on us and how we go, like pink lips in a knotted bow.

Elegy for a Fairy Tale

Ray's mother, splayed and drooping, mutters on their front stoop. She sways, a dying sunflower in frayed denim and a half-tied halter, cigarette guttering, empties winking in the weeds like fireflies.

Ray is eleven. Slippers, pajamas, collared robe, shower-damp curls at his neck. His white-blonde hair needs cutting, but the neighbors can't say he's not clean. *Mama,* he whispers. *Please.*

Her chin lifts, corona of hair shimmering. Gazes at him.

Fuck. You. Ricky, she enunciates. Ray's long-gone father doesn't reply.

I watch, Rapunzel in my tower, crafting curses. *No more mothers. No more witches.* I never wonder what that means.

***

He's fixing his bike in the driveway — three-speed Schwinn, acid green, ape hangers, banana seat, cooler even than my brother's chrome yellow two-wheeler.

Hungover, distracted, she presses the button that raises the garage door. Hops into the car. Reverses.

Thump-bump-crunch.

His scream the loudest sound I've ever heard until

she panics, throws it into drive. Her scream the loudest sound I've ever heard until the fire engines blare down Frey Street. An ambulance dopplers; paramedics leap, genuflect, rise—gone. Bright blood in blonde curls. So loud I have to cover my ears, try not to hear what I wished for.

***

I was eight when you came to my birthday party with an envelope full of pennies as a gift, red-inked wishes looped across the front. My mother said *we can't take that,* and your face changed.

Your mother and mine, blood on blonde. Is rage just despair dressed as a warrior?

Parked in front of my old house, watching neighbors I don't know mow and water. No broken bottles, screams, blood. No ambulances wailing into the chrome yellow afternoon. I cursed our mothers, and the curse worked. *No more mothers, no more witches,* I prayed, and now, there's only me.

To Grandmother's House

Soles of my feet, pink as piggies, my grandmother squeals, grabs my toes, suggests soon they're likely to go into a stew, just as soon as they've cooked enough atop the blacktop of Galena street—the roiling, bubbling river of it, tributaries swimming up everyone's driveway—says her tummy's rumbling, grumbling—

flip-flops tripped off or blistered away, I hop-hop-hop—the ground is lava, the grass green-cool—a postage stamp of relief—*ow ow ow* gasping into *ohhh*—

at Grandma's, there is lemonade. She has air conditioning. Stacks of white-butter bread. A drop-leaf table, a blue-fringe tablecloth, a creamer that *moos* when she tips it—evaporated milk swirls into percolated coffee, lightens it to safety, peanut butter-brown drowns the sour-belly black of the Taster's Choice hole that lives on my mother's countertop—

she's got an ice-box, not a fridge. She's got a cellar, not a basement—she's got hard-cool gray under my feet when I creep down the steep, splintered stair, toward a washing machine that rumbles, bubbles, uneasy as a belly. A woven rope, clothespin-pegged, sags rafter-to-rafter, rub and creak. The clothes she's hung, Grandpa's flannels and pinstripes, wait, square as paper dolls, arms hung down like stop signs.

She's got a back stoop with a linked rubber doormat. She's got an attic full of beautiful cousins, cooing like pigeons under the eaves until one night—deep in the black and small of sleep—one of those beauties wakes up screaming—

fly up the stairs, the child shrieking, belly-burnt, curled like bacon in the sheets, cooking like blacktop, roiling, bubbling—

Quick! Bundle in bedspreads, carry to backseat, cool vinyl, fevered cheek, and every red light run—and the hospital just eyes, blind masks, and cool, gray oblivion—

we wake next day to beauty missing, the night bubbling black behind Grandma's eyes.

I'll hear it the rest of my life, she shivers. One hand lifts a cup, milky as dawn, one clutches her belly, rub and creak. *Like to wake the dead she screamed,* boil and shriek, cook and burn. *Lord, Lord, poor little lamb.* Grandpa's paper-doll arms, stopped in the doorway, hanging like laundry. *Just like to wake the dead.*

Unchanged

My father stops the car
near woods, and we climb
from its metal skin
as twilight lowers her cool palm,
ruffles our hair. Little pinecones
crunch and crush,
above us nightbirds call, respond,

and I write stories in my head,
poems of what they might have said,
like a story I once heard,
that said my soul, all souls, are birds—
things made of magic.

If I open my mouth, the bird flies out.

My body left hollow, ringing
like the singing bowl
my uncle brought home
from mystical Tibet—
better to stay silent.
Keep safe and whole.

We are searching for cicadas.

They leave their skins
stuck to these trees, shells
of the tiny monsters they once were.
Are they unafraid of change,
or unaware?

In the backseat on the way home,
I stick the molts I've found
atop plastic straws, like puppets.
Make them fight.

Like the birds, I make them say
whatever I like; spill their stories,
their poems, until they are hollow.
Empty bodies dancing on sticks.

We are not cicadas,
my father and me.
We crawl back into our shell,
head home, back underground.
We do not sing, or fly away,
or change. We remain.

Monsters.

What Already Could Be Written No More*

My grandfather hunkers,
squats like a toad,
in the stalking forest
where his death begins —
where a hole,
hidden under leaves
and sticks,
is waiting for him.

It's going on dusk now,
soon they will leave,
no prizes, no triumph
to mark the hours
wasted, waiting
in the blind.

The boys are hungry.
Stiff and sore.
Ready for home
and hot showers,
still believing
the worst this day will offer
is the disappointment
of an unspent rifle,
the truck bed empty.
Innocent as fawns,
they holler his name.
His vocation.
Perhaps an incantation,
because

this is the moment
when all it might stop —
though it doesn't stop,
and has never stopped.

My uncle calls out.
My father's whistle cracks
like a shot in the purpling air.
And my grandfather —
again,
and always —
doesn't hear,
or doesn't listen.
Chooses to go on.

The shadow of a buck.
Is that an antler dipping?
So like a tree,
but so like a kill,
and he must follow
where his senses beckon —

the twang of leaf-rot
that stings his nose,
the chumble
of the tiny creek —
white noise
that damps a snort?
A stamp?

Head on a swivel,
cap screens his eyes,
sun sliding egg-yolk-yellow

down the sky,
turning orange as marmalade,
orange as his vest,
creeping forward, one more step
toward the rest
of the rest
of his life—
clicks the safety off,
lifts his foot—
and again,

and forever,

as he always has, always will,

my grandfather chooses
the hole.

*a line by Jacques Dupin, from Songs of Rescue 44,
translated by Paul Auster

Cousinweed

Nobody cared how old I was, because I was a cousin, wasn't I, and fit just fine on the dead-end rail digging into my bony ass under my cut-offs. We passed that joint and they told me about boys at Jones Beach, the way to roll up your skirt so the nuns wouldn't catch you, how to steal sips of communion wine and I kept my mouth shut—silence, my part of the spell. They were tall, and beautiful, like the Kennedy's—straight teeth, shining hair, shining futures, somehow special in a way I couldn't be because, though I was a cousin (wasn't I?), I wasn't blood—made instead from buck teeth, split ends and small, foreign bones. Still, we shared that weed, underhanding a bottle, leaning against the garage, shrinking into the corner where the stinking wisteria climbed the trellis, sneaking glances up the street as they passed stories back and forth about older boyfriends with cars, about what to do with their hands, knees, backseats, black leather jackets, cheap beer. We toked, they talked—college visits, bras, dress fittings—standing on the dais, arms spread like wings, turning like models, like Miss America—the Macy's seamstress humming, chatting around a mouthful of pins while their mother, my Aunt Ronnie, watched and straightened hems and smiled at them in the mirror— we smoked that joint in the summer dust, dusk beginning to peep and chirrup and croak, mosquitoes diving, dopplering around our ears, internal clocks clocking the time, my cousins (?) heading back to Grandma's house and their lives—blue eyeshadow, The Russian Tea Room, boys and beaches. I stayed. Stood in the driveway for another minute, hiding the empty in the tall grass near the garage as the sun bled out over the dead-end rail and tiny white stars, bright as pebbles in a Hansel-and-Gretel world, glittered. Remembering a morning when Aunt Ronnie smoothed the fuzz of my bangs, dusted my shoulders, smiling into the mirror. *Where did you come from, I wonder?* she mused aloud, brushing a crumb from my cheek, her fingers soft, so soft.

Celebration

Lost all night, a familiar city,
houses that I know,
I know —
black powder, bone-ash,
green-smoke, sweet smoke —
home.

My father finds me.
His brain is addled —
he wants to bring me
to my dead grandmother —
he thinks that she'll know
where to find us,
and will come find us,
if I'll just call her,
Why won't you call her?

Because Celebration's wobbling
on the rail that guards the gully,
and I'm holding tight
to the waistband of her jeans —
but her arms are wings,
and joy propels her,
fall or flight.

She's a girl I know, but never met.
Sting of cinnamon, slingshot comets,
horizon to horizon eyes,
dark-soaked sky, fizz and crack
of cans of beer, and here —
what already could be written no more*:

the wet slap of night-thick air,
low jazz buzzing in my hips,
how lips sip salt
from the skin of summer,
and the birds decide
when we sing,
when we sleep—

my father has evaporated.

Wandered off
to find that burning house of bones,
but I am home with Celebration,
as she pops another cream ale top.
Exploding wonder of her mouth
on mine, achieving lift-off
from the dead-end sign.

*a line from Jacques Dupin's <u>Songs of Rescue 44</u>, translated by Paul Auster

Secret Lives of Small Things

I lose things. My glasses, phone, keys. I lose them, and I always have. They slip sideways into a nameless void.

My warm wool sock. One leather glove. Out of my hands, they crawl into a shadow world, find each other there and clasp hands, relieved, saying *I know you. I know you.*

I panic, paralyzed, fingers snaking my hair, unable to move or think. My armpits flood, my mouth dries, I cannot spit or shout. I can only croak, a frog, repeating *Oh, no. Oh, **no**.*

I lose things on the bus, on planes, in other people's homes. I leave them in cafes. In parks when they fall from my pockets.

I lose them, and I am terrified.

They, however, are on vacation.

Unmatched gloves wave to each other. Keys jingle, laughing. A billion pens and pencils dance, leaving an unintelligible scrawl on the void's floor. Scraps of paper covered with phone numbers and passwords talk to each other in the language of numbers: butt dialing, logging into websites and learning about Gobeckli Tepe, dinosaurs, the poetry of Roethke and Rilke. They send prank texts, giggling, and refuse to reveal themselves. All this, while I hyperventilate. Lost, without *them*.

I lose things—but they take pity on me and return. Turn up in a pocket of last year's sweater, between couch cushions, or in my friends' cars, who drive them back to me like an uber service for mislaid umbrellas. And sometimes I look down at the floor and what I lost is sitting innocently in the middle of the carpet, never lost at all.

That's when I groan, pick up my lost, small, important thing and yell at it, like my mother yelled at me, finding me daydreaming under a clothes rack at Sibley's after five long minutes of terror. Scooping me up, squeezing, crying *don't you ever do that again!* my small arms and legs gripping her neck, her rump. Understanding, even then, that I would. Of course I would. I had to.

Galena Street III

I brake at the end of Galena Street, but I don't kill the engine. The car waits, coiled on its haunches, trembling. Blue-bellied clouds writhe overhead, the sky wet, wanting to open.

I loosen my blouse, scoop out my breast, offer it to you like the Host on its paten. You bend to this communion, your tongue rough as a cat's. I arch my back and yowl.

The car shivers like a body. The tail pipe drips sweat. The clouds unzip and flood the street, water whirlpooling over storm sewers, sluicing from the pavement's crumbled edge, waterfalling into the gully. A sheath of raindrops slides over us, hides our ritual, but Galena Street is empty. Driveways deserted. Windows gazing into the distance like dead men. The neighborhood sighs and dreams, a ghost town.

So I stake my claim. Take back what was always mine, the helicoptering maple, the gate in the back fence, the pussy willows at the edge of the Morrisey's yard, their softness sweet against my face. I take back jackrabbit hill, sledding fast on steep ice. The witch that lived on the roof of the playhouse. The purple violet with its single velvet petal. Marilyn, Diane, Erin and Debbie. White-blond Ray Kaya and his alcoholic mother, an envelope of piggy-bank coins the only birthday present he could give. I take back Beverly, her whole family. Her mother, singing Carmen. Her father's swinging briefcase and five o'clock shadow.

I take back my father, the five o'clock savior of sometimes.

The almost-knight in shining armor. Sir Silly Putty, turning Sunday comics into fleshy pink copies of Beetle

Bailey and Li'l Abner. Grandma's Charlie, my daddy, the man that might have been. Almost was. I claim him. I save *him*.

The rain stops. We have finished our prayers, panting in the front seat like flagellates, the spell incanted, the offering made. I roll down my window, breathe the scent of wet concrete sweetening in the sun. Shadows sleep in the gully, as they always will, but the rest of this world is brightening, waking up, ghosts, dreams, and angels steaming from the guardrail, ascendant.

Acknowledgements

"1968," *Alternative Milk Magazine,* forthcoming

"Maps of a World," *Flash Boulevard,* 2025

"God of my Father," *Alternative Milk Magazine,* forthcoming

"Galena Street," *Synkroniciti Magazine,* 2024

"Dirty Summer," *Literally Stories,* 2024

"Christmas Visit," *Litro Magazine,* 2023

"Dream Christine," *Flash Boulevard,* 2024

"The Day and I," *The Rome Review,* 2024

"How We Go," *Does It Have Pockets,* 2025 as "Erasing the Compass"

"Elegy For a Fairy Tale," *Flash Boulevard,* 2025

"To Grandmother's House," *Flash Boulevard,* 2025

"Unchanged," *Synkroniciti Magazine,* 2025

"Cousinweed," *Anti-Heroin Chic,* 2024

"Celebration," *The Rome Review,* 2024

About the Author

Jennifer Maloney has been nominated for the Pushcart Prize, Best of the Net, and Best Small Fictions.

Find her work in Synkroniciti Magazine, Literally Stories, The Magazine of Fantasy & Science Fiction and many other publications. She is the author of *Evidence of Fire, Poems and Stories* (Clare Songbirds Publishing, 2023) and *Don't Let God Know You are Singing, Poems and Stories* (Before Your Quiet Eyes Publishing, 2024).

Jennifer is a parent, a partner, and a very lucky friend, and she is grateful, for all of it, every day.

www.ingramcontent.com/pod-product-compliance
Lightning Source LLC
Chambersburg PA
CBHW020024050426
42450CB00005B/631